The
Try Not To
Laugh Challenge
Joke Book
For Kids and Family

Tickle Your Funny Bone Edition

With Funny Illustrations

Riddleland

Check out some of the fun illustrations that comes with the jokes

More fun illustrations

Table of Contents

Introduction

"Children don't need more things. The best toys a child can have is a parent who gets down on the floor and plays with them." – **Anonymous**

We would like to personally thank you for purchasing this book. The Try Not to Laugh Challenge: Tickle Your Funny Bone edition is different from other joke books. It is not meant to be read alone, but instead it is a game to be played with siblings, friends, family or between two people that would like to prove who is a better comedian. Time to see who has the funny bone in the family!

These jokes are written to be fun and easy to read. Children learn best when they are playing. Reading can help increase that vocabulary and comprehension. They have also many other benefits such as:

- **Bonding** – It is an excellent way for parents and their children to spend some quality time and create some fun and memorable memories.

- **Confidence Building** - When parents give the riddles, it creates a safe environment for children to burst out answers even if they are incorrect. This helps the children to develop self confidence in expressing themselves.

- **Improve Vocabulary** – Jokes are usually written in easy to advance words, therefore children will need to understand these words before they can share the jokes.

- **Better reading comprehension** – Many children can read at a young age but may not understand the context of the sentences. Riddles can help develop the children's interest to comprehend the context before they can share it to their friends.

- **Sense of humor** –Funny creative jokes can help children develop their sense of humor while getting their brains working.

Rules of the Game!

The goal is to make your opponent laugh

- Face your opponent
- Stare at them!
- Make funny faces and noises to throw your opponent off
- Take turns reading the jokes out loud to each other
- When someone laughs, the other person wins a point

The first person to get 5 points, is crowned The Joke Master!

Riddleland Bonus Play

Join our special Facebook Group at
Riddleland For Kids
or
send an email to:
Riddleland@riddlelandforkids.com
and you will get the following

- 50 Bonus Jokes and Riddles
- An Entry in our monthly giveaway of a $25 Amazon Gift card!
- Early access to new books

We draw a new winner each month and will contact you via email or the Facebook group.
Good Luck!

Chapter 1: The Funny Bone Challenge

"There's nothing more contagious than the laughter of young children; it doesn't even have to matter what they're laughing about" – **Criss Jamie**

When his son left the house for college, what did the buffalo tell his son?

Bison!

How can you tell that a dogwood tree is a dogwood tree and not any other tree?

By its bark!

What did the girl ocean say to the boy ocean when he asked her out on a date for the very first time?

Shore.

What cereal do leprechauns like to eat every morning before going to work?

Lucky Charms

What is the one thing that mature chickens and classical music have in common?

Bach, Bach, Bach!

Why was the ripped person who lifts weight for a living mad and upset?

He worked with a bunch of dumbbells.

What was the reason the toddler pony had to go to her room with no dinner or dessert?

She kept horsing around.

What is the hardest match to get out of the tiny matchbox?

A wrestling match!

What did Jimmy say to Ana when she tried to eat his cheese?

Nach-o cheese!

Why should a blind polar bear never, ever operate the remote control for his TV?

He'll keep pressing the paws button.

Why was the hard-working woman fired from her coin factory job?

She had stopped making cents.

At what time does the baby snake get to go into the restaurant for her birthday celebration?

I'm not exactly sure, but she shouldn't be long.

Why did Dracula go into the wrong coffin?

It was an accident because he made a grave mistake.

Why do people say common sense is like deodorant?

It is because the people who need it most, never use it

What is the name of the baby computer's father?

Chip!

What do people in jail use to call their friends back home?

Cell phones!

What street does Mr. Horse lives on?

Mane Street

What is the best season to use the huge trampoline in the back yard?

Spring time!

What is the orangutan's favorite thing about bananas?

They are so appealing!

Why was the girly rubbish bin sad?

Because she was dumped.

What is an American bumble bee named?

USB!

What is a puppy's role in a soccer game?

The ruff-eree

What style does the moon get when he goes to the hair

salon?

Eclipse!

What do you call seagulls that live by the bay?

Bagels!

What kind of witch enjoys the beach the most?

The sand-witch!

What's the first thing the vampire does when he gets

sick?

He immediately starts coffin!

What was the name of the oldest snowman in the world?

Water!

What is the wind's favorite color?

It is blew, of course!

What's the name of the ant that never goes anywhere?

Permanent.

What is the name of the world's fastest flying

policeman?

Mr. Helicopper!

What do you call a sheep without legs?

A cloud

What is the name of a leather belt with a clock on it?

It's called a waist of time!

What did the cozy blanket tell the king-sized bed when he forgot his lunch money?

No problem, friend. I got you covered!

Why is the broom always, always late for work?

He always over-sweeps.

What are the construction workers' favorite sandwich to eat for lunch?

A ham-mer wich.

What is the difference between the newborn baby and the star quarterback?

The baby takes a nap and the quarterback takes a snap!

Why is it important to take a ballpoint pen to the garden?

It's important so you can weed and write!

What's the easiest way to make an egg roll?

Just push it!

What language do billboards use to talk to each other?

They use sign language!

What is a happy rabbit called?

It's called a hop-timist!

What did the two birds in love call each other?

Tweetheart!

What's the name of the woman who had no body, and just a big nose?

Unfortunately, no-body nose!

Why was the cross-eyed teacher fired?

He was fired because he was unable to control his bad pupils!

What argument do the baseball player and the bowler always have?

Their argument is always about when there's a strike!

What cheese is the favorite of all successful basketball players?

Swiss-h cheese!

What method do tall trees use to get on the internet?

They just log-in!

If your grandma is on speed dial, what do you call that?

Instagran!

What are the teenage boulders' favorite rock band?

The Rolling Stones!

Why can't we trust robot spies?

They might have a few screws loose

What did the mommy rabbit say before she and her

family ate dinner?

Lettuce pray!

What's the reason why the nose is in the middle of your

face and not anywhere else?

It is in the middle because it is scent-er!

What do marathon runners do when they forget

something?

They jog their memory!

Why can't the hurricane ever find sunglasses that fit?

It only has one eye!

What did the ghost like to eat during a horror movie?

Ice Scream!

What is a ghost's favorite pair of pants to wear?

Boo jeans!

What did the nail and magnet say to each other?

You're extremely attractive.

What made the leaf go to the doctor?

It was feeling green!

What did the mother bullet say to the father bullet?

Guess what! We're having a BB!

What did the mama broom tell the children brooms?

It's time to go to sweep!

What did the bride at the wedding say when she dropped her beautiful hand bouquet?

Aw, whoopsy daisies!

Why is life similar to a shower?

If you're not careful and make one wrong turn, you're in extremely hot water!

Why couldn't the dinosaur cross the road?

Because there were none!

Why did the skeleton never fight his bully?

He just didn't have the guts!

What was the name of the world's stinkiest fairy?

Her name was Stinkerbell!

What do you call the dentist who specializes in fixing buck alligator teeth?

I don't know, but he is definitely crazy!

What's the zombie's favorite place for vacation?

Death Valley!

When you combine the world's oldest tree and a very smart person together, what do you get?

You get Albert Pine-stein!

What did the dental hygienist give the musician when he left the dentist office?

She gave him a tuba toothpaste!

What is the tree's worst month every year?

It's Sept-timber!

What do you call a very old whale?

A hunch back whale!

What are the ghoul's dad and mom called?

His trans-parents!

How do the children love to travel?

In mini-vans.

What do you get when you cross a bracelet with a pear?

A food chain!

What did the wife bee tell her husband bee when she got home?

Honey, I'm home!

What did the tulips say to the unicycle?

Um, petal!

What's the best thing to put in pie?

A knife and fork!

Why did the pirate parents not let their kids go to the movies?

Because the movie was rated RRRR!

What's the name of the mole's favorite book?

Holes!

Why shouldn't you tell a mirror your favorite joke?

It may just crack up!

Why do barbers make the best drivers?

They know every single shortcut!

How do you make a skeleton laugh?

You tickle its funny bone!

What fruit is the best at gymnastics?

Bananas, because they are great at splits!

What are math teachers' favorite trees to climb?

Geometry!

Why is Cinderella so bad at baseball no matter how much she practices?

Her coach was a pumpkin. That's why!

What is the big foot's favorite meal?

Spayeti!

What is the wizard's favorite subject in school?

Spell-ing!

What do you call unhappy raspberries?

Blueberries!

What's the name of a man who's always running short on time everywhere he goes?

Tim!

What do pickles do on their days off from work?

I'm not sure, but whatever they do, they are sure to relish it!

Where's the best place to plant flowers in a school?

The Kinder-garden!

What are rain clouds wearing under their clothes?

Thunderwear!

Why is the shoe always late for class?

He's always tied up!

What did the people say, who watched the lady fall

while she was ice skating?

They didn't say anything or laugh, but the ice cracked up!

What do you call a jacket that's on fire?

You call it a blazer!

Why did the kid toss butter out the upstairs window?

He just wanted to see the butter fly!

What's the best way to describe any time you go camping?

It's in tents!

Why did my cousin bury all his money in the snow?

To get cold, hard cash, of course!

What is the toad's favorite drink?

Croak-a-Cola!

Why does seaweed live in saltwater?

Because pepper water always makes it sneeze!

What did the rear bicycle tire say to the front bicycle tire when times were getting tough?

Mate, wheel get through this!

Why are traffic lights red all the time?

They always have to change in front of everyone!

What money do the stars use?

They use star bucks!

What do you call a tornado when you say it 10 times fast?

A tongue twister!

Why did the skeleton crash the barbecue party?

He needed a spare rib!

What toy is the rapper's favorite?

The yo-yo-yo!

What is the robot's favorite snack to eat?

Computer chips!

Where do boats go when they are sick?

They visit the dock-ter!

Why does the doctor always seem mad?

He is always losing his patients!

How did the boy feel after he flew his kite in a thunderstorm?

He was very shocked.

Chapter 2 - Animal Jokes

"When we make **Play** the foundation of learning, we teach the Whole child" – Vince Gowmon

What did the potatoes say to the elephant?

Absolutely nothing. Potatoes do not talk!

What is the sound that porcupines make when they kiss

each other?

Ouch!

What do you give a dog that has a bad cough and a fever?

Mustard, it's the best thing for a hot dog!

What did the poor farmer call the cow that had no milk?

"An udder failure"

Why did the chicken Not cross the road?

There was a busy KFC on the other side!

What animal has more lives than a cat?

Bullfrogs, they croak every single night!

What do you call a girl with a frog sleeping on her head?

Lily!

What is the difference between a fish and a guitar?

You can tune a guitar, but you can't tuna fish!

Why do hippos have such big nostrils?

They have big fingers!

What did the flea ask the other flea after they left the

concert?

Should we walk or take a dog?

What is the owl's favorite type of math?

Owl-gebra

Why do scientists think that hummingbirds hum all the time?

Because they can never remember the words!

What did the duck say when she bought lip gloss at the drug store?

Put it on my bill, please!

Why is the barn so noisy at all hours of the day?

All the cows have horns!

Why did the witches' team lose the baseball game that they had practiced very hard for?

All of their bats flew away!

Why can't dinosaurs clap their tails or hands?

Because they are extinct!

What do you call an adult giraffe in a toll booth in Florida?

Stuck!

How do birds love to go on vacation?

They fly.

What did the group of sardines call the packed submarine

that floated by them?

A can full of people!

Why did the overworked elephant leave the world's most

popular circus?

He was tired of working for measly peanuts!

What did the golden retriever tell the flea that was

eating on his ear?

Please stop bugging me!

Why are fish always so easy to weigh no matter what size they are?

They have their own scales!

What happened when two silk worms got in a fight at school?

It ended in a tie!

Why do pandas like old black-and-white movies?

Black and white is relatable for them!

Why did the turkey cross the busy road?

To show everyone that she was not a chicken!

What do you get from a very pampered cow?

Spoiled milk!

What says 'Eoo'?

A cow with no lips!

Why did the T-rex cross the packed road?

No chickens were available!

How can you tell that a rabbit's getting old?

Look for the grey hares!

What is spotted and goes round and round and round and round?

A cheetah in a revolving door!

If you have 5 goats and 20 cows, what do you have?

You have plenty of milk!

What do you call a turtle at the North Pole?

Cold and lost!

What is the name of a big bear that is caught in the pouring rain?

A drizzly bear!

What would happen if pigs could actually fly?

The price of bacon would go up!

What is a beaver's favorite dessert to have after every meal?

Mudcakes!

Why does a giraffe have two long legs?

So they can walk!

What is the cat's favorite breakfast food?

Mice Krispies!

What question did the puppy ask the freshly-baked bread?

Are you pure bred?

What kind of key do you need to open a banana?

A monkey!

How do you take a dog with no legs for a walk?

You don't. You take him for a ride!

Which happens when you cross a baby goat and a baby shark?

I do not know, but I would not milk it!

What is the lion's favorite food?

Baked beings!

How do you stop a dog from digging in your garden?

You take the shovel from him!

Why is the toad one of the happiest animals alive?

They always eat what is bugging them!

What happens when you mix elephants and a fish?

Swimming trunks!

Where does the shark go for their favorite vacation?

Finland!

Why do birds always fly South?

The trip is too long to walk!

What do you call a snake with no clothes?

Snaked!

What do you call a polar bear in the jungle?

Lost!

What is the horse's favorite TV show?

Graze Anatomy!

What do you get when you combine a giraffe and an ant?

A giant!

Why did the gum cross the road?

It was stuck on the bottom of the chicken's foot!

What do whales have that no other mammals have?

Baby whales!

Where do you take a sick horse?

To the horse-pital!

What do you call a polar bear in a store?

Still lost!

What do you give a pig who wins a medal at the Pigs Olympic games?

A pork medallion!

Why are worms the best animals to play poker?

They have five hearts.

What is the difference between a fly and a bird?

The bird can fly but a fly can't bird!

What do you call a funny chicken?

A comedi-hen!

What does a cheetah say when someone glances at it?

Aw man, I have been spotted!

Why did the mama cat move her kittens from the side of the road?

She did not want to litter!

What do you call the bumblebee that is always complaining?

A grumble bee!

What do you call a deaf lion?

It does not matter. It can't hear you!

Where do cows go for culture?

The moo-seum.

Why can't an emu fly?

It can't book a flight.

Why did the turtle cross the road?

To get to the shell station!

What do you get from an angry shark?

As far away as possible!

What do fish take to stay healthy?

They take Vitamin C!

What do you call a skinny cow?

Lean beef!

Two fish are in a tank. What did the first fish say to the second fish?

Do you know how to drive this thing?

What do you get when you cross a cheetah and a snowman?

You get frostbite!

Why was the centipede late for the game?

It had to put all its shoes on!

What do you get when you cross a cheetah and a sheep?

You get a polka dot sweater!

What did the mama cow tell the baby cow?

It's pasture bedtime!

What did the spider do on the computer?

It made a website!

What is the shark's favorite sandwich?

Peanut butter and jellyfish!

How do birds fly?

They just wing it!

Why did the turkey leave the costume party?

Everyone thought he was a boar!

What do you call a rabbit with fleas?

Bugs Bunny!

What kind of snakes are found on cars?

Windshield vipers!

What do ducks like to watch on television?

Duck-mentatries!

What is the dog's favorite city?

New Yorkie!

What happens to the frog's car when it breaks down?

It gets toad away!

Why do cows like jokes?

They like being a-moo-sed!

What part of the chicken makes the most music?

A drumstick!

What kind of ties do pigs wear?

Pig sties!

Why did the policeman give the sheep a ticket?

He was a baaad driver!

What game do elephants play in the back of the car?

Squash!

How many sheep do you need to make a sweater?

I am not sure. I do not think sheep know how to knit!

What kind of dog is all bark and no bite?

A dogwood!

What is a cheetah running a copy machine called?

A copy cat!

What is the bunny's life motto?

Don't worry, be hoppy!

How do you know that carrots are good for you?

You never see a rabbit wearing glasses!

What did the horse say when it fell down?

I fell, and I cannot giddyup!

What kind of bird works at a construction site?

It's called a crane!

What bird is always sad?

A blue jay!

How long should the horse's legs be?

Long enough to reach the ground.

Which side of the horse has the most hair?

Why, on the outside, of course

What do you call a bruise on a T-rex?

A dino-sore!

What is the lion's favorite state?

It's Maine!

Why does the giraffe have such a long neck?

Because his feet stinks!

What can't a camel ride a bike?

They can't find a bike helmet!

What did the porcupine say to the cactus?

Are we related?

What is the alligator's favorite drink?

It's gator-ade.

What do you do if your cat swallows your pencil?

You should just use a pen instead!

How is a dog like a telephone?

It has collar I.D.!

Who makes clothes for the dinosaur?

A dino-sewer!

How did Noah see the animals on the ark at night?

He used flood lighting!

Why do you bring fish to a party?

Because it goes well with chips!

What time is it when 5 dogs chase

Five after one!

Chapter 3 - Wordplay Jokes

"There's nothing like seeing the smile on my kids' faces. Laughing together. Playing. It's the best." – **Mark Wahlberg**

What country does candy come from?

Sweden!

Why did the ice cream cone take karate lessons?

It was tired of getting licked!

What does the cheetah say to his friends before they go out to eat?

Let us prey!

What kind of makeup do ghosts wear?

Mas-scare-a!

Why is the pastry chef mean?

She beats the eggs and whips the cream!

Why did the musician go to time out?

She got in treble.

What is purple and 5000 miles long?

The Grape Wall of China!

What does the baker say to his customers?

Do you oven come in here?

What does the dentist of the year get?

A little plaque!

Why were the pizza vegetables mad?

Because there was not mush room!

What is the definition of illegal?

A large sick bird!

What do you call a girl standing in the middle of the volleyball court?

Annette!

What type of music are balloons scared of?

Pop music!

What is Tarzan's favorite Christmas Carol?

Jungle Bells!

What is a gathering of octopus called?

Octoposse!

What time does the duck wake up?

At the quack of dawn!

How did dinosaurs decorate their bathrooms?

With reptiles!

Why did orange go out with a prune?

He could not find a date!

Where do pepperonis go on vacation?

The Leaning Tower of Pizza.

What did the dalmatian say after dinner?

Ah, that hit the spot!

What makes music on your head?

A head band!

What do you call very scared dinosaurs?

Nervous rex!

What kind of candy bar does an employee crave before the weekend?

A Payday!

Why is a piano so difficult to open?

Because the keys are on the inside!

What did the baker say when the pizza fell on the floor?

Another one bites the crust!

How do you fix broken spaghetti?

You use tomato paste!

Why did the melon jump in the lake?

He wanted to be a watermelon!

What did the lawyer name his daughter?

Sue!

What day do fish hate the most?

Fry-day!

What do a shark and a computer have in common?

They both have megabites!

What do you call purple when it's breaking laws?

Violet!

What animal needs to wear a wig?

A bald eagle does!

What school teaches you to greet people?

Hi school!

What sound does a nut make when it sneezes?

Cashew!

What does the orthodontist do before he rides a

rollercoaster?

He braces himself!

What do you call a cow that is a dictator?

Moosilini!

Why did the girl nibble on her calendar?

She wanted a sundae!

What do elves do after school?

They do their gnome work.

Why did the chef quit his job?

They cut his celery!

How does the volleyball player deliver her messages?

By AirMail!

Why are playing cards like wolves?

They come in packs!

What do sharks say when something cool happens?

Jawesome!

Why did the tomato blush?

Because it saw the salad dressing!

Which superhero hits the most home runs?

Batman!

Why shouldn't you hire a short chef?

The steaks are too high!

Why did coffee file a police report?

It got mugged!

What do you call a sheep covered in chocolate?

A candy baa!

Why are koalas not really bears?

Because they do not meet the koalafications!

Why didn't anyone care about the circus?

Because it was irr-elephant!

Where do cows go on holiday?

Moo Zealand

Which animal does Russian milk come from?

Moscows!

What do you call a pile of cats?

A meow-tain!

What do you call cows with a sense of humor?

Laughing stock!

What kind of bees eat brains?

Zombees!

Did you hear about the guy who got a tattoo of an

octopus?

He got inked up!

What is it called when a bull lies about other bulls?

It's called bullying!

What did the cow say when it saw the farmer twice in one day?

It said, "Deja moo!"

What does a cat say when it's angry?

Please stop stressing meow-t!

What do you get when you cross a pig and a pineapple?

A porky pine!

What is the only school where you have to drop out to graduate?

Skydiving school!

Why did the banana go to the hospital?

It was not peeling very well!

How did the octopus to go war?

Well armed!

What animal gets easily offended?

Chickens because they are always getting roasted!

What do you call a magic owl?

Hoo-dini!

Did you hear about the shellfish that could play the violin really well?

It has excellent mussel memory!

What do cows eat for breakfast?

Steer cereal!

What kind of table can you eat?

A vege-table!

What is a pig's favorite ballet?

Swine lake!

What do cows like to do?

They like to cow-culate!

Why can't you tell a joke standing on ice?

Because it might crack up!

What does my dog do when he goes

He reads a bite-time story!

What do you call a pig with no legs?

A groundhog!

Why didn't Cinderella make the basketball team?

She ran away from the ball!

Where do you put barking dogs?

In the barking lot!

What did the trees wear to the pool?

Swimming trunks!

Why did the otter cross the street?

To get to the otter side!

What do you call an octopus that fights sharks?

Octobrave!

Where do mummies go swimming?

The Dead Sea.

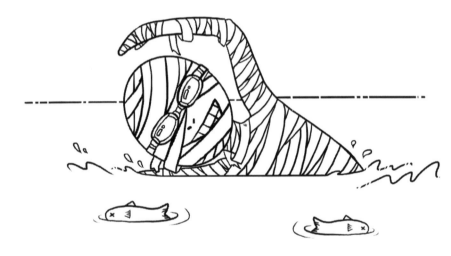

What do you get when you combine a parrot and

centipede?

A walkie-talkie!

What dance do all astronauts know how to do?

The moonwalk!

What music do ghosts dance to?

Soul music!

What do you call a group of peppers dancing?

Salsa.

Why did Pam go to the lake after her cousins teased her?

She wanted to fish for compliments!

What kind of berry likes coloring books?

A crayon-berry!

Why did the soccer ball shout?

Because a man kicked him!

Why can't chefs play baseball well?

They are always caught trying to steal basil

Why didn't the scary skeleton go to the fancy dance?

He had no body to dance with!

Why did the soccer player bring string to the game?

So she could tie the score!

How do athletes stay cool during a game?

They stand near the fans!

What does a cowboy eat before a rodeo?

Bullogna!

What do bees need in order to fly in the rain?

Their yellow-jackets!

What type of footwear do spies wear?

Sneakers!

What did the egg say to his funny friend?

You really crack me up!

What kind of dog chases anything red?

A bulldog!

What is grey and then turns red?

An embarrassed hippo!

What is the pig's favorite color?

It's mahogany!

Why are spiders great volleyball players?

They have an excellent top spin

Why did the deer need braces?

He had buck teeth!

Why did the volleyball player join the army?

They wanted to serve our country!

What do you call a goat with a beard?

A goatee!

How do you spell mousetrap?

C-A-T!

What did the lonely checkerboard say?

I am board!

Where do all the crayons love to go for vacation?

Color-ado!

Why did the girl bring lipstick and eye shadow to her classroom?

She had a makeup exam!

What game do all the chefs want to win?

The Hunger Games.

What game do fish like to play?

Salmon Says!

What vegetable loves to lift weights?

A muscle sprout!

What is King Arthur's favorite game?

Knights and crosses!

What is the chef's favorite thing to do?

Cut the cheese!

What did the dentist say to the computer?

This will not hurt a byte.

Chapter 4: Knock-Knock Jokes

"Play builds the kind of free-and-easy, try-it-out,

do-it-yourself character that our future needs."

~ James L. Hymes, Jr

Knock! Knock!

Is there someone out there knocking on the door?

Yup, me, Minty teeth!

Really? Minty teeth who?

Sorry for the smell, I meant to brush my teeth!

Ring! Ring!

May I know who's on the other line, please?

Why? It's your mother!

Your mother who?

No, it's your mom, not a knock-knock joke. And you

better not hang up on me!

Ding! Dong!

Who's out there, please?

Your friend, Richie!

I do not know anyone by that name. Richie who?

Richie, why didn,'t you come to the door? It's taking you too long. It's cold out here!

Beep! Beep!

Is someone honking the car outside?

Yup, it's your girl, Lisa!

Oh yeah? Lisa who?

It's the Lisa I could do to get your attention!

Vroom! Vroom!

Is someone driving my brand new car?

Yup, it's your friend, Lucy!

Are you sure? Lucy who?

Lucy the steering wheel. Park the car and turn it off. You're too young to drive!

Click! Click!

Who's taking my picture without my permission?

It's Ken!

Really? Ken who?

Ken you smile please? I just want a good shot with you

smiling.

Knock! Knock!

Hey! Who is at the door knocking loudly at this hour?

I am a new friend, Jill!

Really? Jill who?

Jill who went up the hill with Jack!

Chirp! Chirp!

What is out there in the night trying to scare me?

It's me, darkness!

Hmm, darkness who?

Please let me in. I can't see!

Bang! Bang!

Who's knocking this loudly at my back door?

Your best friend, Winston!

You sure? Winston who?

The Winston blew right through my jacket!

Knock! Knock!

Hello, who is banging at the door?

It's me, Jim!

Jim who?

Jungle Jim!

Brriing! Brriing!

May I ask who's calling, please?

Sure thing. It's Dusty!

Um, Dusty who?

A-choo! Someone needs to clean up in here! It's too Dusty.

Ding! Dong!

Who's trying to get in from the cookout?

Do not play. It's me, Frank!

Really now? Frank who?

The kind you eat with mustard and ketchup!

Knock! Knock!

Who is there, please?

It's your friend, Billy!

I do not recall knowing a Billy. Billy who?

Can you Billy-eve it? I am finally here!

Buzz! Buzz!

Hey! Who's ringing my doorbell this early in the morning?

It's me, Aria!

I do not know an Aria. Aria who?

Aria tired of asking who it is yet?

Chirp! Chirp!

Who is calling me, please?

Your great friend, Percy!

I do not know a Percy. Percy who?

Percy, your long-lost friend that you never knew you had!

Ring! Ring!

Who's calling me this early in the morning?

It's your best friend, Earl!

Are you sure? Earl who?

Yup, Earl-y bird gets the worm!

Ring! Ring!

Tell me who's speaking on the other line?

It's Finger!

Um, er, um, Finger who?

Finger foods! Yum! Yum!

Ding! Dong!

Who's knocking at my door, please?

It's Froggy!

I am not too sure I know you. Froggy who?

Are you not hoppy to see me?

Knock! Knock!

Tell me who is there, please?

It's me, Toe!

What? Toe who?

You're asking Toe many questions! Let me in.

Beep! Beep!

Is someone there right now?

Yup, it's Someday!

What kind of name is that? Someday who?

Someday, you'll be glad that you opened the door!

Brriing! Brriing!

Who's calling me right now?

You know. It's me, Hannah!

I do not know. Hannah who?

When I get to your house, can you give me a Hannah

with my homework?

Buzz! Buzz!

Who's that buzzing?

The name's fruit fly!

Really? Fruit fly who?

Fruit does not fly!

Ring! Ring!

Who's calling me?

It's me, Leak!

Hmm, you sure? Leak who?

You better clean up this leak before someone falls!

Ring! Ring!

Who is it ringing my cell?

You know me. It's Open book!

Really? Open book who?

Surprise! Open-book test! You have 10 minutes to finish it.

Beep! Beep!

Who is beeping me on my beeper?

Your good friend, Miles!

Help me out here. Miles who?

Do not worry about it. I am Miles away!

Buzz! Buzz!

Can you tell me your name, please?

You know me. It's Misa!

Really now? Misa who?

I will Misa you when you get off the phone!

Chirp! Chirp!

Who's calling me now?

It's your friend, Orange!

Really? Orange who?

Orange you going to remember me? How can you forget your best friend!

Bang! Bang!

Who's there knocking at the door?

It's your friend, Don!

Help me remember you please. Don who?

Don, Don, Don—the friend who saves you before the monster!

Riiiing! Riiiing!

Is someone ringing my doorbell right now?

Yup! Please open the door. It's Bug!

Hmm, Bug who?

Please do not Bug me.

Buzz! Buzz!

Who is calling me now?

It's me, your favorite friend A!

You sure about that? A who?

Let's hang out today. We'll have A-hoot!

Brriing! Brriing!

Who's ringing my bell right now?

It's me, Pecan!

What? Pecan? Pecan who?

Pecan someone your own age!

Brriing! Brriing!

Who's ringing my bell so loudly?

It's me, Marty!

What? Marty? Marty who?

Do not be a Smarty Pants!

Buzz! Buzz!

Who's buzzing my doorbell?

Hey, it's Pamela!

I do not know a Pamela, so Pamela who?

Why are you screaming so loudly?

Bang! Bang!

Who's banging on my door this late at night?

It's me, Scrambled eggs!

Scrambled eggs who?

I would like my eggs scrambled well with cheese please!

Knock! Knock!

Who is on the other side of the door?

You know me. It's Happy and you know it!

I am not sure who that is. Happy and you know it who?

If you're happy and you know it, clap your hands!

Ring! Ring!

Hello, who is this?

It's Peek-a-boo!

Really? Peek-a-boo who?

Peek-a-boo, I see you!

Ding! Dong!

Who's there? Hey, who's there?

Someone who can't reach the doorbell!

Buzz! Buzz!

Who's calling my line at this time?

It's me. Your favorite state Tennessee!

Yes? Tennessee who?

The only Ten-you-see!

Knock! Knock!

Excuse me, who's there?

You know me. It's Luke!

You sure? Luke who?

Oh, Luke what you made me do!

Buzz! Buzz!

Who is buzzing me right now?

It's me, Audrey!

You sure? Audrey who?

Are you not Audreym come true?

Bang! Bang!

Who's there, please?

It's me, Christmas tree!

Um, Christmas tree who?

Oh, Christmas tree, how lovely are your branches!

Knock! Knock!

Who is knocking so hard on my door?

You know me, it's Randy!

Nope, I do not know a Randy. Randy who?

I Randy the entire house twice!

Ding! Dong!

Who's at the door please?

It's me, Tess!

You sure? Tess who?

Do not Tess me. Open the door.

Ring! Ring!

Hello, who's calling me?

Please! It's me, Broken needle!

You sure about that? Broken needle who?

Never mind, there's no point!

Buzz! Buzz!

Hello, who's there?

It's me, Zen!

I do not know a Zen. Zen who?

Is Zen-y body home?

Brriing! Brriing!

Hey there! May I know your name, please?

Sure thing. It's Vin!

Really? Hmm, Vin who?

Vin are you going to let me come in?

Knock! Knock!

Who's there at the door?

It's me, an important person named Hustle!

That is a strange name. Who is Hustle?

Hustle up something to eat, why don't ya? I am hungry!

Chirp! Chirp!

Who is there, please?

It's me, Force!

Um, I do not know a Force. Force who?

May the Force be with you!

Ding! Dong!

May I know who is there, please?

You sure can. It's Chip!

Really? Chip? Chip who?

Chip in, and give me a hand, why don't ya?

Ring! Ring!

Hello, who's there?

The name's Courtney!

Tell me more. Courtney who?

Courtney last time. Let me in.

Buzz! Buzz!

Who's buzzing me today?

It's me, Flo!

Really? Flo who?

If you do not let me in, I am going to Flo.

Bang! Bang!

Who's there knocking so loud at my door?

It's me, Better!

Really? Better who?

Better open up fast. It's chilly out here.

Brriing! Brriing!

Howdy, who's there?

It's me, Howie!

Really? Howie who?

Howie still not friends on Instagram?

Chirp! Chirp!

Can you let me know who's there?

It's Tammy!

Are you sure? Tammy who?

Tammy what we're going to do today!

Knock! Knock!

Who's at my front door, please?

You know. It's me, Tag!

Really? Tag who?

Tag, you're it!

Ding! Dong!

Who's ringing my bell right now?

It's me, First!

Are you sure? First who?

First, open the door, and I can tell you more.

Ding! Dong!

Who wants to come in?

You know me, Tia!

Nope. Tia who?

Tia be or not to be, that is the question!

Ring! Ring!

Hello, who's there?

You know me. It's Wa!

Wa Who?

Yay, I did not know you were that happy to see me!

Ring! Ring!

Who's there?

It's me, Cheesy!

What kind of name is that? Cheesy who?

A Cheesy slice of pepperoni pizza!

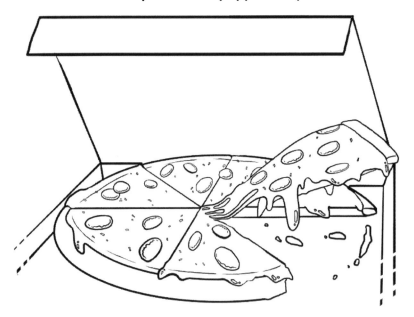

Buzz! Buzz!

Who wants to come in right now?

Please let me in. It's me, Hugs!

Huh? Hugs who?

Hugs and kisses!

Brriing! Brriing!

Who's on the line?

Your favorite person, Chocolate!

I do not know anyone by that name. Chocolate who?

Do not be choco-late for school today!

Knock! Knock!

Please let me know who's there?

It's me, Joe!

Not ringing a bell. Joe who?

Joe-body!

Chirp! Chirp!

Who's calling me at this time?

It's me, Russ!

Really now? Russ who?

Open the door. Do not be a Russ!

Buzz! Buzz!

Who's there, please?

It's your neighbor Ivan!

Are you sure? Ivan who?

Ivan missing you.

Did you enjoy the book?

If you did, we are ecstatic. If not, please write your complaint to us and we will make sure to fix it.

If you're feeling generous, there is something important that you can help me with - tell other people that you enjoyed the book.

Ask a grown-up to write about it on Amazon. When they do, more people will find out about the book. It also lets Amazon know that we are making kids around the world laugh. Even a few words and ratings would go a long way.

If you have any ideas or jokes that you think are super funny, please let us know. We would love to hear from you. Our email address is - **riddleland@riddlelandforkids.com**

Scan the QR code using your camera app on your phone to be directed to the review page.

Alert: Riddleland Bonus Play

Join our special Facebook Joke Group at
~Riddleland For Kids~

or

send an email to:

Riddleland@riddlelandforkids.com

and you will get the following

- 50 Bonus Jokes and Riddles
- An entry in our monthly giveaway of $25 Amazon Gift card!
- Early Access to new books

We draw a new winner each month and will contact you via email or the Facebook group.
Good Luck!

Would you like your jokes and riddles to be featured in our next book?

We are having a contest to see who are the smartest or funniest boys and girls in the world!

1) Creative and Challenging Riddles
2) Tickle Your Funny Bone Contest

Parents, please email us your child's "Original" Riddle or Joke, and he or she could win a $50 Amazon gift card and be featured in our next book.

Here are the rules:

1) It must be challenging for the riddles and funny for the jokes!

2) It must be 100% original and not something from the Internet! It is easy to find out!

3) You can submit both a joke and a riddle as they are 2 separate contests.

4) No help from the parents unless they are as funny as you.

5) Winners will be announced via email or our Facebook group – Riddleland for kids

6) Please also mention what book you purchased.

7) Email us at Riddleland@riddlelandforkids.com

Other Fun Children's Books for Kids!
Riddles Series

Encourage your kids to think outside of the box
with these Fun and Creative Riddles!

Get them on Amazon

Try Not to Laugh Challenge Series

Would You Rather... Series

Get them on Amazon

or our website at www.riddlelandforkids.com

About Riddleland

Riddleland is a mom + dad run publishing company. We are passionate about creating fun and innovative books to help children develop their reading skills and fall in love with reading. If you have suggestions for us or want to work with us, shoot us an email at riddleland@riddlelandforkids.com

Our family's favorite quote

"Creativity is an area in which younger people have a tremendous advantage since they have an endearing habit of always questioning past wisdom and authority." – Bill Hewlett

Printed in Great Britain
by Amazon